This F###$&@! Book Belongs to:

_____

name

site address

username

password

notes

name

site address

username

password

notes

name

site address

username

password

notes

name

site address

username

password

notes

A

name

site address

username

password

notes

name

site address

username

password

notes

name

site address

username

password

notes

name

site address

username

password

notes

name
site address
username
password
notes

name
site address
username
password
notes

name
site address
username
password
notes

name
site address
username
password
notes

A

name _____
site address _____
username _____
password _____
notes _____
_____
_____

name _____
site address _____
username _____
password _____
notes _____
_____
_____

name _____
site address _____
username _____
password _____
notes _____
_____
_____

name _____
site address _____
username _____
password _____
notes _____
_____
_____

name

site address

username

password

notes

name

site address

username

password

notes

name

site address

username

password

notes

name

site address

username

password

notes

B

name
site address
username
password
notes

name
site address
username
password
notes

name
site address
username
password
notes

name
site address
username
password
notes

name

site address

username

password

notes

name

site address

username

password

notes

name

site address

username

password

notes

name

site address

username

password

notes

name
site address
username
password
notes

name
site address
username
password
notes

name
site address
username
password
notes

name
site address
username
password
notes

name
site address
username
password
notes

name
site address
username
password
notes

name
site address
username
password
notes

name
site address
username
password
notes

name _____
site address _____
username _____
password _____
notes _____
_____
_____

name _____
site address _____
username _____
password _____
notes _____
_____
_____

name _____
site address _____
username _____
password _____
notes _____
_____
_____

name _____
site address _____
username _____
password _____
notes _____
_____
_____

name

site address

username

password

notes

---

name

site address

username

password

notes

---

name

site address

username

password

notes

---

name

site address

username

password

notes

name

site address

username

password

notes

name

site address

username

password

notes

name

site address

username

password

notes

name

site address

username

password

notes

name

site address

username

password

notes

name

site address

username

password

notes

name

site address

username

password

notes

name

site address

username

password

notes

name

site address

username

password

notes

___

name

site address

username

password

notes

___

name

site address

username

password

notes

___

name

site address

username

password

notes

___

name

site address

username

password

notes

name

site address

username

password

notes

name

site address

username

password

notes

name

site address

username

password

notes

name

site address

username

password

notes

_____

_____

name

site address

username

password

notes

_____

_____

name

site address

username

password

notes

_____

_____

name

site address

username

password

notes

_____

_____

name
site address
username
password
notes

name
site address
username
password
notes

name
site address
username
password
notes

name
site address
username
password
notes

name
site address
username
password
notes

name
site address
username
password
notes

name
site address
username
password
notes

name
site address
username
password
notes

name

site address

username

password

notes

name

site address

username

password

notes

name

site address

username

password

notes

name

site address

username

password

notes

E

name
site address
username
password
notes

name
site address
username
password
notes

name
site address
username
password
notes

name
site address
username
password
notes

name

site address

username

password

notes

name

site address

username

password

notes

name

site address

username

password

notes

name

site address

username

password

notes

name

site address

username

password

notes

name

site address

username

password

notes

name

site address

username

password

notes

name

site address

username

password

notes

name

site address

username

password

notes

name

site address

username

password

notes

name

site address

username

password

notes

name

site address

username

password

notes

name

site address

username

password

notes

name

site address

username

password

notes

name

site address

username

password

notes

name

site address

username

password

notes

name

site address

username

password

notes

name

site address

username

password

notes

name

site address

username

password

notes

name

site address

username

password

notes

name

site address

username

password

notes

name

site address

username

password

notes

name

site address

username

password

notes

name

site address

username

password

notes

name

site address

username

password

notes

name

site address

username

password

notes

name

site address

username

password

notes

name

site address

username

password

notes

name

site address

username

password

notes

name

site address

username

password

notes

name

site address

username

password

notes

name

site address

username

password

notes

name

site address

username

password

notes

name

site address

username

password

notes

name

site address

username

password

notes

name

site address

username

password

notes

H

name

site address

username

password

notes

name

site address

username

password

notes

name

site address

username

password

notes

name

site address

username

password

notes

name
site address
username
password
notes

name
site address
username
password
notes

name
site address
username
password
notes

name
site address
username
password
notes

name

site address

username

password

notes

name

site address

username

password

notes

name

site address

username

password

notes

name

site address

username

password

notes

name

site address

username

password

notes

name

site address

username

password

notes

name

site address

username

password

notes

name

site address

username

password

notes

name

site address

username

password

notes

name

site address

username

password

notes

name

site address

username

password

notes

name

site address

username

password

notes

name
site address
username
password
notes

name
site address
username
password
notes

name
site address
username
password
notes

name
site address
username
password
notes

name
site address
username
password
notes

name
site address
username
password
notes

name
site address
username
password
notes

name
site address
username
password
notes

name

site address

username

password

notes

name

site address

username

password

notes

name

site address

username

password

notes

name

site address

username

password

notes

name
site address
username
password
notes

name
site address
username
password
notes

name
site address
username
password
notes

name
site address
username
password
notes

name
site address
username
password
notes

name
site address
username
password
notes

name
site address
username
password
notes

name
site address
username
password
notes

J

name
site address
username
password
notes

name
site address
username
password
notes

name
site address
username
password
notes

name
site address
username
password
notes

name

site address

username

password

notes

---

name

site address

username

password

notes

---

name

site address

username

password

notes

---

name

site address

username

password

notes

K

name

site address

username

password

notes

name

site address

username

password

notes

name

site address

username

password

notes

name

site address

username

password

notes

name

site address

username

password

notes

name

site address

username

password

notes

name

site address

username

password

notes

name

site address

username

password

notes

K

name

site address

username

password

notes

---

name

site address

username

password

notes

---

name

site address

username

password

notes

---

name

site address

username

password

notes

name
site address
username
password
notes

name
site address
username
password
notes

name
site address
username
password
notes

name
site address
username
password
notes

name
site address
username
password
notes

name
site address
username
password
notes

name
site address
username
password
notes

name
site address
username
password
notes

name
site address
username
password
notes

name
site address
username
password
notes

name
site address
username
password
notes

name
site address
username
password
notes

L

name

site address

username

password

notes

name

site address

username

password

notes

name

site address

username

password

notes

name

site address

username

password

notes

name
site address
username
password
notes

name
site address
username
password
notes

name
site address
username
password
notes

name
site address
username
password
notes

name
site address
username
password
notes

name
site address
username
password
notes

name
site address
username
password
notes

name
site address
username
password
notes

name

site address

username

password

notes

name

site address

username

password

notes

name

site address

username

password

notes

name

site address

username

password

notes

name
site address
username
password
notes

name
site address
username
password
notes

name
site address
username
password
notes

name
site address
username
password
notes

name

site address

username

password

notes

name

site address

username

password

notes

name

site address

username

password

notes

name

site address

username

password

notes

name

site address

username

password

notes

name

site address

username

password

notes

name

site address

username

password

notes

name

site address

username

password

notes

name

site address

username

password

notes

---

name

site address

username

password

notes

---

name

site address

username

password

notes

---

name

site address

username

password

notes

name

site address

username

password

notes

___

___

name

site address

username

password

notes

___

___

name

site address

username

password

notes

___

___

name

site address

username

password

notes

___

___

name

site address

username

password

notes

name

site address

username

password

notes

name

site address

username

password

notes

name

site address

username

password

notes

name

site address

username

password

notes

name

site address

username

password

notes

name

site address

username

password

notes

name

site address

username

password

notes

name

site address

username

password

notes

name

site address

username

password

notes

name

site address

username

password

notes

name

site address

username

password

notes

name

site address

username

password

notes

name

site address

username

password

notes

name

site address

username

password

notes

name

site address

username

password

notes

name
site address
username
password
notes

name
site address
username
password
notes

name
site address
username
password
notes

name
site address
username
password
notes

name
site address
username
password
notes

name
site address
username
password
notes

name
site address
username
password
notes

name
site address
username
password
notes

name

site address

username

password

notes

name

site address

username

password

notes

name

site address

username

password

notes

name

site address

username

password

notes

P

name
site address
username
password
notes

name
site address
username
password
notes

name
site address
username
password
notes

name
site address
username
password
notes

name
site address
username
password
notes

name
site address
username
password
notes

name
site address
username
password
notes

name
site address
username
password
notes

name

site address

username

password

notes

name

site address

username

password

notes

name

site address

username

password

notes

name

site address

username

password

notes

name

site address

username

password

notes

---

name

site address

username

password

notes

---

name

site address

username

password

notes

---

name

site address

username

password

notes

name
site address
username
password
notes

name
site address
username
password
notes

name
site address
username
password
notes

name
site address
username
password
notes

name
site address
username
password
notes

name
site address
username
password
notes

name
site address
username
password
notes

name
site address
username
password
notes

name
site address
username
password
notes

name
site address
username
password
notes

name
site address
username
password
notes

name
site address
username
password
notes

name

site address

username

password

notes

---

name

site address

username

password

notes

---

name

site address

username

password

notes

---

name

site address

username

password

notes

name
site address
username
password
notes

name
site address
username
password
notes

name
site address
username
password
notes

name
site address
username
password
notes

name
site address
username
password
notes

name
site address
username
password
notes

name
site address
username
password
notes

name
site address
username
password
notes

R

name
site address
username
password
notes

name
site address
username
password
notes

name
site address
username
password
notes

name
site address
username
password
notes

name
site address
username
password
notes

name
site address
username
password
notes

name
site address
username
password
notes

name
site address
username
password
notes

S

name

site address

username

password

notes

---

name

site address

username

password

notes

---

name

site address

username

password

notes

---

name

site address

username

password

notes

name
site address
username
password
notes

name
site address
username
password
notes

name
site address
username
password
notes

name
site address
username
password
notes

S

name

site address

username

password

notes

_____

_____

name

site address

username

password

notes

_____

_____

name

site address

username

password

notes

_____

_____

name

site address

username

password

notes

_____

_____

name
site address
username
password
notes

name
site address
username
password
notes

name
site address
username
password
notes

name
site address
username
password
notes

S

name

site address

username

password

notes

name

site address

username

password

notes

name

site address

username

password

notes

name

site address

username

password

notes

name

site address

username

password

notes

---

name

site address

username

password

notes

---

name

site address

username

password

notes

---

name

site address

username

password

notes

name
site address
username
password
notes

name
site address
username
password
notes

name
site address
username
password
notes

name
site address
username
password
notes

name
site address
username
password
notes

name
site address
username
password
notes

name
site address
username
password
notes

name
site address
username
password
notes

name
site address
username
password
notes

name
site address
username
password
notes

name
site address
username
password
notes

name
site address
username
password
notes

name

site address

username

password

notes

name

site address

username

password

notes

name

site address

username

password

notes

name

site address

username

password

notes

name

site address

username

password

notes

---

name

site address

username

password

notes

---

name

site address

username

password

notes

---

name

site address

username

password

notes

name

site address

username

password

notes

name

site address

username

password

notes

name

site address

username

password

notes

name

site address

username

password

notes

name

site address

username

password

notes

name

site address

username

password

notes

name

site address

username

password

notes

name

site address

username

password

notes

name
site address
username
password
notes

name
site address
username
password
notes

name
site address
username
password
notes

name
site address
username
password
notes

name
site address
username
password
notes

name
site address
username
password
notes

name
site address
username
password
notes

name
site address
username
password
notes

name

site address

username

password

notes

name

site address

username

password

notes

name

site address

username

password

notes

name

site address

username

password

notes

V

name
site address
username
password
notes

name
site address
username
password
notes

name
site address
username
password
notes

name
site address
username
password
notes

name
site address
username
password
notes

name
site address
username
password
notes

name
site address
username
password
notes

name
site address
username
password
notes

name

site address

username

password

notes

name

site address

username

password

notes

name

site address

username

password

notes

name

site address

username

password

notes

name

site address

username

password

notes

name

site address

username

password

notes

name

site address

username

password

notes

name

site address

username

password

notes

name _____
site address _____
username _____
password _____
notes _____
_____
_____

name _____
site address _____
username _____
password _____
notes _____
_____
_____

name _____
site address _____
username _____
password _____
notes _____
_____
_____

name _____
site address _____
username _____
password _____
notes _____
_____
_____

name

site address

username

password

notes

name

site address

username

password

notes

name

site address

username

password

notes

name

site address

username

password

notes

name

site address

username

password

notes

name

site address

username

password

notes

name

site address

username

password

notes

name

site address

username

password

notes

name

site address

username

password

notes

---

name

site address

username

password

notes

---

name

site address

username

password

notes

---

name

site address

username

password

notes

X

name
site address
username
password
notes

name
site address
username
password
notes

name
site address
username
password
notes

name
site address
username
password
notes

name

site address

username

password

notes

_____

_____

name

site address

username

password

notes

_____

_____

name

site address

username

password

notes

_____

_____

name

site address

username

password

notes

_____

_____

name

site address

username

password

notes

name

site address

username

password

notes

name

site address

username

password

notes

name

site address

username

password

notes

name
site address
username
password
notes

name
site address
username
password
notes

name
site address
username
password
notes

name
site address
username
password
notes

name

site address

username

password

notes

name

site address

username

password

notes

name

site address

username

password

notes

name

site address

username

password

notes

name

site address

username

password

notes

name

site address

username

password

notes

name

site address

username

password

notes

name

site address

username

password

notes

name
site address
username
password
notes

name
site address
username
password
notes

name
site address
username
password
notes

name
site address
username
password
notes

name

site address

username

password

notes

_____

_____

name

site address

username

password

notes

_____

_____

name

site address

username

password

notes

_____

_____

name

site address

username

password

notes

_____

_____

name

site address

username

password

notes

name

site address

username

password

notes

name

site address

username

password

notes

name

site address

username

password

notes

name

site address

username

password

notes

---

name

site address

username

password

notes

---

name

site address

username

password

notes

---

name

site address

username

password

notes

name

site address

username

password

notes

name

site address

username

password

notes

name

site address

username

password

notes

name

site address

username

password

notes

Manufactured by Amazon.ca
Bolton, ON

21597125R00063